BEFORE I MADE HISTORY™

W9-APM-513

TURN ON THE LIGHT, THOMAS EDISON!

BY PETER AND CONNIE ROOP

SCHOLASTIC INC.

New York   Toronto   London   Auckland   Sydney
Mexico City   New Delhi   Hong Kong   Buenos Aires

ISBN 0-439-43927-2

10 9 8 7 6 5 4   5 6 7 8/0

Printed in the U.S.A.   40
First printing, February 2003

For Peter, a hands-on wizard in his own right!

TABLE OF CONTENTS

INTRODUCTION

Thomas Edison liked to experiment. Do you know how old he was when he did his first experiment, with goose eggs?

Thomas Edison invented the lightbulb. Did you know that he failed hundreds of times before he succeeded in creating the lightbulb?

Thomas Edison invented the first phonograph. Did you know he was partially deaf and could barely hear music?

Thomas Edison repeated a nursery rhyme into his first phonograph. Do you know what nursery rhyme he said?

Thomas Edison had many accidents. Did you know he almost died from one?

Thomas Edison loved to learn new things.

Did you know that a teacher thought he could not learn?

Thomas Edison only had three months of schooling. Do you know who his favorite teacher was?

Thomas Edison loved to read. Did you know he read every book in an entire library?

Thomas Edison loved railroads and trains. Did you know he almost caused a terrible train wreck?

Thomas Edison invented more than a thousand things during his lifetime. Do you know how old he was when he made his first invention?

The answers to these questions lie in who Thomas Edison was as a boy and as a young man.

This book is about Thomas Edison before he made history.

1

THOMAS EDISON IS BORN

February 11, 1847. Snow swirled around a small brick house in Milan, Ohio. A raging blizzard blew off Lake Erie. An oil lamp glowed in the "birthing room" where babies were born.

Suddenly, the outside door opened, and in rushed Dr. Galpin. It was three o'clock in the morning, and his help was desperately needed. A baby was about to be born.

Soon the baby snuggled with his tired mother, Nancy Edison. He had deep blue eyes and light brown hair. His mother wrapped him in a blanket she had decorated with a shell pattern. Mrs. Edison had spent three hours every day knitting the blanket so her baby would be warm.

Samuel Edison wrote the baby's name at the bottom of the birth page in the Edison family Bible. He wrote in tiny letters because the page had been filled with many other Edison names.

Thomas Alva Edison
February 11, 1847.

Thomas was named after his great-uncle Thomas. His middle name, Alva, was in honor of Captain Alva Bradley, a close family friend.

Thomas would have had six older brothers and sisters, but three had died during the harsh Ohio winters. Their names were Carlisle, Samuel, and Eliza. His two sisters, Marion (age eighteen) and Tannie (age thirteen), and his brother, Pitt (age fifteen), heard Thomas cry that night. Nancy and Samuel Edison hoped Thomas would survive.

Dr. Galpin was worried, though. Thomas had an unusually large head. He thought Thomas had a fever in his brain. Samuel and Nancy were puzzled by their son's big head.

His father thought something was wrong with Thomas. His mother, however, felt his large head was a sign of intelligence.

His father, sisters, and brother called Thomas by his middle name, Alva. His mother, however, called the baby by her pet name for him, Al.

Al brightened up his family's world. He was unusually quiet, and he rarely cried. He giggled and laughed. Al laughed for the joy of laughing, almost as if he knew something no one else knew. A friend said, "Even as a baby, Al cracked jokes."

All his life, Thomas Alva Edison made people feel good. He changed their lives. But no one had any idea on that snowy February morning just how many lives Thomas Alva Edison would change.

2

AL'S EARLY DAYS

The Edison house stood at the top of a steep hill. A canal at the bottom connected Milan with Lake Erie and the wide world beyond. In spring, the canal was busy with hundreds of ships loading wheat, corn, cattle, hogs, and lumber for faraway cities.

Samuel Edison had grown up in Canada. He believed Milan would be an important city, so he moved his family there. Samuel owned a factory that made roof shingles. The factory also supplied wood for homes, warehouses, and ships.

Samuel Edison had built his family's house. He split the roof shingles and made the floorboards. Samuel built the house so well that today it still stands as solid as it did on the day Thomas Edison was born.

The top floor had two bedrooms, one for the children and one for the parents. The middle floor had a sitting room, a parlor, and the birthing room, where Thomas was born. The bottom floor was cut into the hillside. Here was the warm kitchen where Mrs. Edison cooked, used her spinning wheel to make thread, washed her family's clothes, and kept an eye on eager, active Al.

Al was curious. He observed his family's busy world. He watched Pitt draw pictures and Tannie write. He watched Marion make her wedding dress and his mother do her chores.

When Al was two years old and could walk, he went everywhere. He played in the yard, and he wandered into the nearby woods. He explored the house. Al watched ships in the canal being loaded with farm products. Al enjoyed the sounds of busy Milan: workmen shouting, sailors singing, wagons rumbling, horses snorting, saws buzzing, and blacksmiths hammering. Al especially enjoyed birds singing.

When he was three years old, Al began running his fingers through his hair as he watched and listened. For the rest of his life, Thomas Edison ran his fingers through his hair when he concentrated.

Al liked to copy things. When Pitt practiced his drawing, Al drew pictures, too. Before he knew letters, Al copied signs.

Al liked to wander with his father to the town square. He listened to men tell stories, and he stared into store windows. His father treated Al to peppermint candies.

Sometimes, Al wandered off alone to explore the world. His unhappy mother or angry father searched for him.

They found Al down by the canal. They found him building with wood scraps in the lumberyard. Al might be singing songs with sailors or watching sparks fly from a blacksmith's hammer.

Al's mother kept a switch behind her kitchen clock. A switch is a long, thin rod used for whipping. She did not like to switch Al. But she wanted to teach him to not wander away. Mr. Edison spanked Al, too.

One day, when Al was three years old, his mother could not find him. She looked down the hill. No Al. She called his name. No answer. She heard wagons rumbling. Finally, she found Al staring at the brightly colored wagons rolling down the street.

These wagons carried families, not grain. They were rolling west, hoping to strike it rich in the California gold rush. Al wanted to climb onto a wagon to see where it was going.

All his life, Thomas Edison remembered those colorful wagons. "This was my first impression of a great world beyond," he said.

Wherever he was, Al asked questions. He was eager to understand how the world worked.

"Where does the wind come from?

"How high is the sky?

"What makes sparks?"

Mr. Edison lost patience with Al's con-

stant questions. One man said to Mr. Edison, "It would save time to hire a man special to answer your young one's questions."

Mrs. Edison did not mind Al's questions. She admired his imagination and encouraged Al's curiosity. She saw how he observed things and enjoyed his wonder at the world. Nancy Edison knew Al was unique.

Al knew his mother was special, too. Thomas Edison said, "I was always a careless boy. But her [his mother's] firmness, her sweetness, her goodness, were potent powers to keep me in the right path." Al knew his mother believed in him, even if she did have to switch him sometimes for his own good!

3
AL GETS INTO
TROUBLE — BIG TROUBLE

Al's curiosity got him into trouble. One day, when Al was two, he visited his sister Marion. She was married and lived on a farm outside Milan.

Al wandered into the barn to see what he could see. He watched a hen sitting on her nest and was amazed when chicks hatched from her eggs. Al had an idea! He would experiment and would make goose eggs hatch.

Al gathered goose eggs and put them in a nest. Then he sat on the nest. Al sat and sat. Nothing happened.

Al heard someone shouting, "Little Al,

…ere are you?" Suddenly, the barn door flew open. Marion's husband, Homer, rushed in.

Homer saw Al sitting on the nest. He laughed.

"Did you fall in and make a nice omelet?" Homer asked.

"I didn't fall in," answered Al. "I thought I could make little gooses come out of goose eggs if I sat on them. If the hens and geese can do it, why can't I?"

"Wait until your sister sees the seat of your pants!" Homer exclaimed.

Marion hugged Al instead of spanking him. She said, "Al, you did a very smart thing, even if it didn't work. If no one ever tried anything, no one would ever learn anything. Maybe someday you'll try something that will work."

Another time, when he was about five years old, Al climbed to the top of a grain elevator. He slipped and fell, and down he tumbled into the slippery grain. Al struggled. He did not want to smother in the grain. Fortunately, a worker rescued Al.

Mr. Edison spanked Al that night. Al took his punishment, but he did not stop being curious.

That same year, Al was in the barn. He wanted to see how fire burned, so he lit a small fire. But the fire quickly grew bigger and bigger. Soon the barn was burning!

When the fire was out, Mr. Edison marched Al to the town square. No spanking at home. This time Al was punished in public. But even this punishment did not end Al's curiosity.

Later that year, Al tried another experiment. He knew birds ate worms. He knew birds could fly. So he mashed worms into water. He talked a neighbor girl into drinking the mixture so she could fly, too. The girl got sick. Al was punished.

When Al was puzzled and thinking hard, he tugged on his right eyebrow. He had this habit all his life.

Milan was changing. A railroad had been built nearby, but not to Milan. Farmers shipped their products on trains instead of ships. Business in Milan slowed down so much that Samuel Edison decided it was time to move.

When Al was seven years old, the Edisons packed their belongings and moved to Port Huron, Michigan. Al was excited. A new town meant new adventures and new experiences.

A wagon took the Edisons to the train station. Al was thrilled to be speeding along at twenty miles an hour on the train! He enjoyed the fifty-mile ride aboard the steamship *Ruby*. The *Ruby* carried the Edisons from Detroit up the Saint Clair River to Port Huron.

Port Huron was a growing town. New stores were being built, and the sandy streets were being paved with cobblestones. Saws whirled at the sawmills. Al's new home was surrounded by ten acres of woods where he could roam.

But before Al explored his new world, he got very sick with scarlet fever. His parents worried that Al might not live. His mother tenderly nursed Al. He rested, listened to his mother read, and practiced drawing as he recovered. His fight with scarlet fever damaged Al's hearing.

Mr. Edison ran a lumber and grain business. One day he had an idea. He would build a tall tower. People would pay to climb it and enjoy the view. Mr. Edison's tower stood one hundred feet tall. Al stood at the bottom and collected twenty-five cents from each visitor. Al and his mother also climbed the tower to read, talk, and gaze at the world.

One day, when he was eight years old, Al found a bumblebee nest. He was curious to know what the inside of the nest looked like. Suddenly, Al was hit from behind and knocked down. He looked back. An angry ram had his head down, ready to butt Al again. Al scrambled over a fence just as the ram charged. Al's mother treated his many cuts and bruises.

That same year, his parents decided that their curious son was ready for school. They hoped that in school Al would learn self-control as well as reading, writing, and arithmetic.

4
AL'S SCHOOLING

Al went to a school that had one room. The students ranged in age from five to twenty-one years old. Al did not like school. He had to memorize dates and math facts. Al would rather ask questions than memorize things.

Al's teacher did not like Al's constant questions. He did not like Al taking naps in class or drawing pictures when he was bored. One day, his teacher lost his patience with Al. Al heard him tell someone he thought Al was addled. Addled means mixed up in the head. The teacher said Al should not be in school.

Later in his life, Thomas Edison said, "I was so hurt by this last straw that I burst out crying and went home and told my mother about it."

Mrs. Edison disagreed with the teacher. Angrily, she marched to school and told the teacher that he didn't know what he was talking about. She added that Al had more brains than the teacher. Mrs. Edison said she would teach Al at home! Thomas Edison's time in school lasted only three months.

Mrs. Edison was an excellent teacher. She did not want Al's mind cluttered with facts, so she did not make him memorize things. She read books to him. They talked about nature. They climbed Edison's Tower. Mrs. Edison answered Al's questions as best she could. When she didn't know the answer, they looked in a book.

Al became an eager reader. He rarely went anywhere without a book tucked in his pocket. Al learned so much at home that by the time he would have been in fourth grade, he was reading college books.

Al's favorite book was about science experiments. Al also enjoyed the *Dictionary of*

Science, another book filled with experiments. Carefully following directions, Al built a machine to make electricity from friction. His second experiment made electricity from a magnet. Thomas Edison was fascinated with electricity the rest of his life.

Al experimented in his room. He collected metal, wire, jars, and bottles. With his allowance, he bought chemicals, batteries, beeswax, and magnets. His mother gave him flour, sugar, and salt. Al mixed different ingredients together. His experiments bubbled. They smelled. They leaked onto the carpet. They exploded!

Finally, Mrs. Edison lost patience with the mess in Al's bedroom. She ordered the experiments to end.

Al had an idea. If he cleaned up the basement, could he have a corner for his laboratory? He begged his mother. Mrs. Edison reluctantly agreed, but only if Al put a lock on the door. Al was ten years old when he moved his lab to the basement.

Al experimented in his lab day and night.

He missed meals. He no longer climbed the tower. He missed sleep. Al discovered he didn't need as much sleep as other people. He could take a quick nap and be refreshed.

Mr. Edison wanted Al to read something other than chemistry books. He offered Al money for each book he read that wasn't about experiments. Al needed the money to buy supplies, so he read late into the night. With the pennies he earned, Al bought more chemicals.

When he was eleven years old, Al tried another flying experiment. He knew gas made balloons soar into the sky. He would make a gas that would make a person fly!

Al mixed a special powder with some water. He did not want to try it himself, so Al talked his friend Michael Oates into try-ing it. Michael asked how he would get back down if he started to fly. Al told him to grab a tree branch. Al would get a ladder to help Michael down.

Michael was not sure, but Al was his best friend. Michael drank it. He flapped his arms. He fell down with a horrible stomachache. Al was switched by his mother.

Mrs. Edison was upset about the strange smells coming from Al's lab. She told him that he couldn't have a lab anymore. Al begged and begged. Again, his mother gave in. Al was not to do dangerous experiments. He must label his two hundred jars of chemicals so nobody could get sick.

Al did as he was told. He knew what was in every jar, so Al wrote POISON on each one. He decorated them with skulls and crossbones just to make sure.

In 1996, scientists digging in the basement of the Edison house found jars and bottles left over from Al's laboratory.

5

MORE EXPERIMENTS

Al became fascinated with the telegraph. The telegraph used electricity to send messages along wires. The messages were sent in Morse code, a system of dots and dashes. A dot is a short burst of electricity. A dash is a longer burst. A combination of dots and dashes stood for each letter.

The messages were sent by tapping a telegraph key that made the dots and dashes. Telegraph messages were called "lightning writing" and were the fastest messages people had ever been able to send.

When he was eleven years old, Al built his own telegraph machine from brass. He strung wire from tree to tree between his house and a friend's house. Al needed electricity to send messages. He looked in a book and discovered that he could make electricity by rubbing the fur on a cat backward. Al found two cats, hooked up their back legs to his wire, and rubbed their fur. The two cats did not like Al's idea. They spit at him, and they clawed him. Then they ran to safety.

Instead, Al used a battery for electricity. Soon, Al and his friend were slowly sending and receiving messages. The telegraph worked well until the day a cow ran into the wire and ruined their telegraph system. But Al had other experiments to try.

Al needed more money to buy supplies. He and Michael Oates (Michael was still Al's friend) dug a large garden and planted onions, cabbages, lettuce, corn, beans, and peas. They weeded, hoed, watered, and harvested their crop. Al and Michael pulled a wagon around town, selling their vegetables.

Farming was hard, hot work. That fall, Al

had money for more supplies. He even had enough to give some to his mother.

When he was twelve years old, Al visited his sister Marion again. The railroad now reached Port Huron. Al rode the train to Detroit and then to Milan.

At the end of Al's visit, Mr. Edison came to bring him home. They were taking many crates back with them. Al noticed that the boxes and crates were not well labeled. He found a brush and paint. Carefully, Al labeled the crates.

The stationmaster was so impressed with Al's work that he offered him a job. He would pay Al thirty dollars a month, feed him, and give him a room if he would work for the railroad. Mr. Edison said Al was too young to be away from home. The idea of working on the railroad stayed with Al.

Later that year, Al learned that the railroad needed a newsboy to sell papers to customers traveling from Port Huron to Detroit and back. Al begged his parents to let him have this job. He promised to spend his free time in Detroit reading at the library. Mrs. Edison reluctantly agreed. She worried that Al might be killed in a train wreck. But she knew that when Al made up his mind to do something, nothing could stop him. Al got the job!

6

WORKING ON THE RAILROAD

Al was called a "news butch." He sold newspapers, candy, fruit, peanuts, postcards, books (he read them first), magazines, sandwiches, soap, tea, coffee, and sugar. When the train reached Detroit, Al bought more newspapers and other supplies to sell on the return trip. Then, the day was his to enjoy.

Al wandered the streets of Detroit, the biggest city he had ever seen. He gazed at the buildings, and he stared in the shop windows. He pestered workmen with questions.

Al remembered the promise he made to his mother to go to the library, where he explored the world of books. He said, "I started with the first book on the bottom shelf and went through the lot, one by one. I didn't read a few books, I read the library."

Al had started selling newspapers when more people began reading them. The Civil War had begun in 1861. People were anxious to find out war news. They were especially interested in the lists of soldiers killed or wounded. Every day, Al sold many newspapers.

One day, when he was thirteen, Al stopped by the *Detroit Free Press* to buy newspapers to sell. The paper was throwing out the old lead letters used to print the paper. To his surprise, Al was given the letters, ink, and paper, too! Al would print his own newspaper!

He found an empty space in the baggage car on the train. There, Al printed his *Weekly Herald* newspaper. Al printed changes in the train schedules. He wrote stories and jokes, and he sold ads. He wrote about babies being born and people retiring. When printing on the swaying train proved too difficult, Al

moved his newspaper into his basement workshop.

Al's *Weekly Herald* cost three cents. He often sold four hundred copies of his newspaper a day. He made enough money to pay his mother a dollar a day.

In 1996, scientists digging in the basement of the Edison house also found 185 pieces of the type Al used to print his newspaper.

Al used the space in the baggage car for more experiments. One day, when Al was thirteen years old, an experiment set the baggage car on fire!

Mr. Stevenson, the conductor, threw all of Al's equipment off the train. Then he boxed Al's ears before throwing him off the train, too.

Al felt something snap inside his head. Mr. Stevenson had damaged Al's eardrums. Al's ears had already been hurt when he had scarlet fever. Mr. Stevenson hurt his ears even more. Now Al was almost deaf! He said that after that experience he "could not hear a bird sing." This unfortunate accident changed the path of Thomas Edison's life.

When he was fourteen years old, Al decided he wanted to be called Tom. Tom liked being around the train stations, particularly at Mount Clemons, near Port Huron. Mount Clemons was a busy place.

Mr. MacKenzie, the stationmaster at Mount Clemons, liked Tom Edison. He enjoyed the boy's curiosity and often let Tom listen to the loud clicks of the telegraph.

One day, when he was fifteen, Tom was at the station. Mr. MacKenzie's three-year-old son, Jimmie, was playing in the gravel along the tracks. He did not see a train coming, but Tom did!

Tom sprinted to Jimmie, grabbed him, and together they tumbled off the tracks. The grinding steel wheels missed both boys. Jimmie was crying, but he only had a few cuts. Tom had cuts, too.

Mr. MacKenzie wanted to reward Tom, but he didn't have any money. Knowing that Tom was fascinated with the telegraph, he offered to teach him how to be a telegraph operator. This was Tom's dream come true!

Mr. MacKenzie taught Tom for three months. Tom's goal was speed. He knew Morse code, and he wanted to be fast and accurate in sending and receiving messages.

Tom discovered that because he was almost deaf, he had to feel the sounds with his fingers. He found that his ear problems blocked out noise so he could concentrate harder.

Soon, Tom was able to write forty-five words per minute in Morse code. When Tom had mastered the telegraph, he wanted a job using his new skill. Fortunately, Mr. Walker, a storekeeper, needed someone to work in his store, where Western Union had a telegraph machine.

7
TOM WANDERS AND WONDERS

Tom liked Mr. Walker's store. He sold books, clocks, watches, china, rifles, organs, and science magazines. When Tom wasn't busy with the telegraph, he was free to read and think. Wanting to improve himself, Tom learned how to read faster by grouping words together.

After dinner, Tom returned to the store to receive more messages on the telegraph. When he was not working, reading, or thinking, Tom took naps on a cot.

Tom liked working at night. Since he didn't need much sleep, he could work at night and read and experiment during the day. Thomas Edison had this habit all his life.

Whenever he could, Tom rode in the train engines. He watched engineers work the gauges. He observed the firemen keeping the steam up in the boiler. He asked questions.

One day, fourteen-year-old Tom was riding in the engine of a freight train. The engineer and fireman were sleepy, so they told Tom he could run the engine while they took naps.

Tom ran the train for twenty miles when, suddenly, a shower of muddy ash and black soot exploded from the smokestack. Tom was covered in black soot from head to foot!

The explosion didn't wake up the engineer or the fireman. Tom kept the train going. Then, the smokestack belched ash and soot a second time. Tom, the dirty engineer, safely took his train all the way to town!

Tom grew bored with his work in Mr. Walker's store. He wanted more of a challenge and more pay. While he was looking for a new job, Tom's skills as a telegrapher came in handy.

The winter of 1864, when Tom was sev-

enteen years old, was especially bitter. Ice on the Saint Clair River broke the telegraph cable connecting Port Huron with Sarnia, Canada. The ice was so thick that even the ferryboats could not cross. The two towns could not communicate.

Tom had an idea. A train could be parked by the river on the Port Huron side. The train engineer could then blow his whistle in Morse code.

The long and short blasts of the whistle quickly got the attention of the people in Sarnia. They had a train come down on their side of the river. Before long, the two engines were whistling messages back and forth between the United States and Canada.

Tom's fast thinking got the attention of the railroad owners. When Tom applied for a telegrapher's job seventy-five miles away, in Stratford Junction, Canada, the railroad owners gave it to him.

Tom worked from seven at night until seven in the morning. These hours suited

Tom perfectly. Even better, he would be paid twenty-five dollars a month!

At first, his parents were reluctant to let Tom leave home, but they knew they could not stand in his way. Besides, the Edisons were from Canada, and Stratford Junction wasn't very far away.

Tom packed his few belongings and moved to Canada. He was pleased to be on his own and worked hard at his new job, becoming a skilled "Knight of the Telegraph Key."

But as usual, Tom's attention wandered once he had mastered something. The long nights were very boring when there weren't many messages. Each night, at certain times, a signal was sent to Tom to make sure he was awake. Tom knew when the signal was coming, so he asked the night watchman to wake him if he was sleeping.

One night the signal came, but the night watchman failed to wake Tom. A freight train came roaring down the track from one direction. Another train rumbled from the opposite direction. The two trains barely missed crashing into each other. Tom was immediately fired.

He went home in disgrace. He only stayed a little while, however, because he soon found another job on a different railroad, in Adrian, Michigan. Tom's skills were so valuable that he could get a job almost anywhere. Now he was paid seventy-five dollars a month.

Once again, Tom liked the night shift. He stayed in Adrian for a few months, then moved to Fort Wayne, Indiana. He worked there for six months before moving to Indianapolis, Indiana. Then, Tom left the railroads to work for the Western Union Telegraph Company.

8

TOM THE TELEGRAPHER

Tom was always trying to send messages faster and faster. Even when he wasn't on duty, Tom stayed at work to practice and to watch other telegraphers at work.

Then, Tom had an idea. He would put two telegraph machines together to help make sure the messages were correct. The first telegraph would tap a message onto a piece of paper. The second machine would "read" the dots and dashes and sound them out at a slower speed. This invention made sure that telegraphers would not make mistakes when sending fast messages. This was Tom's first of many improvements on the telegraph.

Tom continued to try to improve his speed in taking telegraph messages. Sometimes these messages came at forty words a minute, and he had to be careful to not make any mistakes. Inventive as usual, Tom created his own type of handwriting. Tom's writing was a mixture of cursive and print. Many of the letters stood straight up. The smaller the letter, the better, Tom thought. All the rest of his life, Thomas Edison wrote in his own unique handwriting.

For the next three years, Tom worked at different telegraphing jobs around the country. All the while, he read and studied and made improvements to the telegraph. He found a way to make the telegraph send and receive messages at the same time.

Tom was paid more money for his skills. As usual, he spent little money on food or lodgings. He bought science books, and he spent money on experiments. He worked especially hard on his electricity experiments.

Tom dreamed of someday not having to work at any job. Instead, he would work on his experiments.

The wandering and late nights took their toll on Tom, and he got sick. In 1867, when he was twenty years old, Tom returned home to Port Huron. He spent the winter recovering and dreaming.

One day, a letter came from his friend Milton Adams. Milton and Tom had once worked together. Milton asked Tom to join him in Boston. Milton told Tom he could get him a telegrapher's job in Boston, but only if he came quickly. Tom packed his bags and caught the first train to Boston.

When he reached Boston, Tom went to the Western Union office. The manager asked him when he could start working.

"Now," Tom answered.

The manager asked Tom to work the night shift. Night work was perfect for Tom.

The other telegraph operators decided to trick Tom. They telegraphed the fastest operator in New York City and told him Tom was new and to send him fast messages.

The New York man started slowly, then

got faster and faster. Tom's fingers flew across the paper as he accurately wrote the message. The New York operator began mixing up words. Suddenly, Tom realized a joke was being played on him.

Tom sent this message to the other operator: *Say, young man, change off and send with your other foot.*

Everyone laughed — Tom had made the trick backfire. They knew Tom was one of the best telegraphers in America.

Tom worked, read about electricity, and experimented. He slept very little. Tom told his friends, "I have got so much to do and life is so short — I am going to hustle." And hustle he did!

Tom joined a group of young men who were also interested in experimenting and inventing. Tom was twenty-one when he invented a special machine for counting votes. He applied for a patent on his invention on October 11, 1868. A patent means that the invention was Tom's, and no one else could copy it without his permission.

The voting machine was Thomas Edison's first patented invention. Unfortunately, no one liked Tom's voting machine. Tom made a promise to himself. He would never again invent anything unless someone had a need for it.

9

TOM INVENTS

Tom lived cheaply, ate little, dressed in wrinkled clothes, slept four hours a night, and spent his money on experiments. One invention paid off. People who owned stock shares in companies wanted to know how well their companies were doing. They wanted to know when stock prices changed. Someone had invented a stock ticker to quickly report stock prices. Tom took this idea and improved it. His invention worked so well that people paid him for it.

In 1868, Tom had a terrible accident. He spilled some acid on his face. Tom quickly washed his eyes out, but the acid still burned. For two weeks, Tom was blind. Fortunately, his sight returned completely.

Before long, Tom grew tired of Boston. It was time to move again. This time he would go to New York, the biggest, busiest city in America. He was twenty-two years old.

Tom arrived in New York in 1869, with no job and a few pennies. But he was determined to make his way in the world. He was so poor and hungry that he begged for a dollar from a friend. Tom wanted the most food for his money. He went to restaurants and ordered apple dumplings. They were cheap and filling. Tom had never eaten anything so good. For the rest of his life, Thomas Edison enjoyed apple dumplings.

A friend let Tom sleep on the floor of the Gold Indicator Company. Tom watched others work while he waited for a telegrapher's job. He studied the machines that telegraphed the price of gold.

One day, the special gold machine broke down, and no one knew how to fix it. Everyone panicked. They had to know the price of gold, or they would lose customers. Tom calmly went to the machine, fixed a broken spring, and the gold machine clicked back to life. The next day the owner of the company gave Tom a job for three hundred dollars a month!

Tom enjoyed his work, but he kept inventing, too. He improved his stock ticker machine. The president of Western Union liked Tom's improved stock ticker so much that he wanted to buy it. Tom didn't know how much to ask for his invention. He thought maybe he should ask for five thousand dollars. No, Tom decided that was too much. Maybe three thousand dollars? The president offered him forty thousand dollars! Tom said, "I never came so near fainting in my life."

The company president wrote Tom a check for forty thousand dollars. A banker cashed the check but paid Tom in dollar bills. Tom stuffed bills into his pockets and stayed up all night guarding his money. In the morning, Tom opened his first bank account.

With the money, Tom quit his job and

opened his own factory to make his stock ticker machines. He hired people to help him. Then Tom built his own laboratory in Menlo Park, New Jersey, where he could experiment day and night.

Tom improved the telegraph, and he improved the typewriter. He hired more workers. Before long, Tom had forty-five new inventions. Tom was called the Wizard of Menlo Park.

One of Tom's workers was Mary Stilwell. Tom fell in love with Mary. On Christmas Day, 1871, Tom and Mary were married. They named their first son Thomas. His father nicknamed him Dot for the Morse code signal. He called his daughter Marion, Dash. Their third child was named William, but Tom called him Willie.

While Tom was busy inventing, so were many others, including Alexander Graham Bell. Bell invented the telephone. Tom took this invention and improved it so voices could be heard better. Because he was partially

deaf, improving sounds was one of Tom's goals.

Tom began experimenting with a way to record voices. His idea was to speak into a mouthpiece with a needle attached onto the end. The vibrations of his voice in the mouthpiece would make the needle scratch a piece of rotating tinfoil. Then, if he put the needle onto the scratch made by his voice and rotated the tinfoil backward, the vibrations would come out of the mouthpiece and his voice would be repeated.

Tom made the machine. Into the speaker, he shouted, "Mary had a little lamb. Its fleece was white as snow. And everywhere that Mary went, the lamb was sure to go."

Then he played it back. Out came Tom's voice: "Mary had a little lamb."

Tom smiled. His workers shouted. Tom had invented the phonograph.

10

TOM LIGHTS THE WORLD

Tom became famous around the world for inventing a talking machine. He was even invited to the White House to meet President Rutherford B. Hayes!

Tom was paid more and more for his inventions. He worked even harder. This was difficult for his wife and children. He forgot to come home for meals. He stayed awake late at night, inventing new things people could use.

From 1878 to 1879, Tom spent much of his time inventing an inexpensive lightbulb. He knew it would be powered by electricity. The hard part was to find something that would give off light but not burn up. Tom tried thin pieces of copper and other metals.

They did not work. He tried weeds, bamboo, wood splinters, fishing line, pieces of cotton, and human hair. Tom tried three thousand ideas before he solved the problem.

Tom took thread and burned it into black carbon. At first, the thread broke when he tried to put it into a bulb. Finally, on October 21, 1879, Tom got a piece inside a glass bulb. Tom wired the bulb to his electrical current. The lightbulb glowed! Tom expected the light to go out, but it didn't! The light burned all night. Tom's helpers stared at the bulb with him. It burned the next day and the next. The first electric light glowed for forty hours!

Tom's electric lights made him even more famous. People from around the world came to see him. Tom's inventions provided him with more money. He said, "I always invent to obtain money to go on inventing."

In 1884, Tom's wife, Mary, died. He was left with Dot, Dash, and Willie. In 1885, Tom met beautiful Mina Miller, the daughter of a fellow inventor. Tom taught the Morse code

to Mina. Later that year, Tom tapped a Morse code message to Mina: "Will you marry me?"

Mina tapped back, "Yes."

On February 24, 1886, Tom and Mina were married. They had three children: Madeleine (born in 1888), Charles (1890), and Theodore (1898).

Thomas Edison kept inventing for the rest of his life. He invented motion pictures. He improved batteries and made cement stronger. Close to his death, he was trying to invent a new kind of tire rubber from goldenrod plants.

On October 18, 1931, Thomas Edison's life flickered out. He was eighty-four years old.

Over his lifetime, Tom invented thousands of new things and improved many more. Who could have imagined how much Thomas Edison would change the world when he was born that snowy night in 1847?